NATIONAL GEOGRAPHIC
KiDS

BRAiN CANDY

2

EXTRA CHEWY!

Seriously Sweet Facts
to Satisfy Your Curiosity

NATIONAL GEOGRAPHIC
WASHINGTON, D.C.

HAVE YOU EVER WONDERED ...

Fact-alicious!

... JUST HOW STRONG A SPIDERWEB IS?

... WHAT RAIN ON OTHER PLANETS LOOKS LIKE?

... WHICH FOODS ARE THOUGHT TO BRING GOOD LUCK?

WELCOME TO *BRAIN CANDY 2*, AN AMAZINGLY APPETIZING ASSORTMENT OF JUICY TIDBITS, TELLING TRUTHS, UNCANNY CONNECTIONS, AND MIND-BLOWING FACTS.

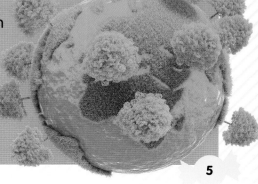

Each spread in *Brain Candy 2* will give you some information and then add to it with related revelations. Millions of particles and debris orbit Earth. Just how big is this space party? About 20,000 pieces are larger than a softball and about 500,000 pieces are larger than a marble! Tornadoes on Earth are powerful, reaching wind speeds of 300 miles an hour (483 km/h), but tornado speeds on the sun are 620 times faster. And guess what? There are more than 300 trillion trees on Earth. That's quite a lot of shade—especially when you learn that it equals about 400 trees for each person on the planet.

LIKE LEARNING COOL FACTS AND HOW THEY'RE CONNECTED? *BRAIN CANDY 2* IS GOING TO BE A TREAT.

SOME ANIMAL **TEETH** ARE

ENORMOUS!

ONE **AFRICAN ELEPHANT TUSK** CAN **WEIGH** MORE THAN **50 POUNDS** **(23 KG),** WHICH IS HEAVIER THAN **TWO LARGE WATERMELONS.**

A **NARWHAL'S** **SWORDLIKE TOOTH,** OR TUSK, IS **LONGER THAN TWO GOLF CLUBS** PLACED END TO END.

A **HIPPO'S CANINE TEETH** CAN GET **AS BIG AS 1.5 FEET** (0.5 M)— THE LENGTH OF **TWO AND A HALF BANANAS!**

Some modern INVENTIONS are actually ancient.

Time for a CATNAP!

THE **ANCIENT GREEKS** INVENTED THE **ALARM CLOCK** AROUND 400 B.C. BY CREATING A MECHANISM THAT DROPPED PEBBLES ONTO A GONG.

ANCIENT EGYPTIANS CREATED A PELLET MADE OF HERBS, SPICES, AND HONEY THAT THEY CHEWED TO FRESHEN THEIR BREATH—MUCH LIKE TODAY'S **MINTS.**

THE **FIRST ROCKETS** WERE DEVELOPED AS FIREWORKS IN **CHINA** IN THE 1200S.

SCIENTISTS THINK **ROMAN EMPEROR NERO** WATCHED GLADIATORS FIGHT USING AN EMERALD AS A **CORRECTIVE EYE LENS.**

SPIDERWEBS ARE SUPER STRONG...

A **SPIDER'S WEB** is strong enough to **CATCH BIRDS AND BATS** that accidentally fly into it.

The **DARWIN'S BARK SPIDER'S WEB** is **TOUGHER THAN KEVLAR,** which is used to make bulletproof vests.

A **SINGLE SPIDERWEB STRAND** is made up of **THOUSANDS OF TINY NANOSTRANDS.**

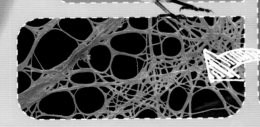

...AND EVEN MORE AMAZING THAN SPIDER-MAN'S!

I'm the **REAL** superhero!

Spiders can transform **liquid** protein **into a solid** strand faster than **3.5 feet a second** (1 m/s).

Some **spiderwebs** can span an **entire river.**

A spider can **fling its web** to float up to **three miles** (4.8 km) **above Earth's surface** or 1,000 miles (1,609 km) out to sea.

The **golden orb-weaver spider** can produce up to **28 different** kinds of silk threads.

See how **CUTE** I am?

Jumping spider

14

NOT-SO-SCARY SPIDERS

Spiders are man's best friend. Really, you ask?
They won't play fetch or cuddle on the couch—in fact, they prefer to avoid humans. (Perhaps because they've been on Earth longer than we have—their ancestors lived before the dinosaurs!) But spiders protect farms by killing and eating insects such as aphids and caterpillars that destroy fruits, vegetables, and grains. They also defend homes from insect invasions, eating cockroaches, flies, and disease-carrying pests like mosquitoes. But that's not all—studies of spiders and their whimsical webs have also advanced human technology. Understanding spider silk's unmatched combination of strength and toughness—and the proteins a spider produces to spin its silky webs—has helped scientists improve everything from medicine to bulletproof vests to repairing ligaments in knees, elbows, and jaws. So if arachnophobia—a fear of spiders—ever strikes, just remember that these insect predators are ultimately human protectors.

Bulletproof vest

A **DOUBLE RAINBOW** IS **DOUBLY SPECIAL.**

16

It occurs when sunlight is **reflected** **twice** inside of **a raindrop.**

The colors on the **second** **rainbow** appear in reverse order.

In **some cultures,** seeing a double rainbow is a **sign of future success.**

DOGS CAN BE HEROES.

It's a RUFF job...

During a snowstorm, a dog **DUG A 200-FOOT** (61-m) **TUNNEL UNDER FALLEN TREES AND SNOW** and dragged his owners to safety.

Frida the Labrador retriever has **RESCUED 52 PEOPLE** in various **NATURAL DISASTERS**, including a **7.1 magnitude earthquake** in Mexico.

Some dogs can **SENSE DANGER**, saving their owners from **fainting, snake attacks,** or **tsunamis.**

FUNGI CAN GET FUNKY ... AND FREAKY!

THE **BLEEDING TOOTH FUNGUS** OOZES A RED LIQUID THAT LOOKS **LIKE BLOOD.**

A PATCH OF **SHOESTRING FUNGUS** CAN GROW UP TO **FOUR SQUARE MILES** (10 SQ KM).

CHICKEN OF THE WOODS IS A BRIGHT ORANGE-AND-YELLOW FUNGUS THAT SOME SAY **TASTES LIKE CHICKEN.**

EVERY YEAR,

18 BILLION POUNDS (8 BILLION KG)

OF **PLASTIC**

ENTER THE **WORLD'S OCEANS.**

THAT'S THE **WEIGHT** OF ...

40,000
STATUES OF LIBERTY.

194 *TITANICS*.

45,000
BLUE WHALES.

Gettin' my
SLIME
on ...

24

THERE'S PLENTY OF GOO TO GO AROUND.

A TEASPOON OF
HAGFISH SLIME
GROWS **10,000** TIMES BIGGER IN ONLY HALF A SECOND, DISORIENTING PREDATORS.

NUDIBRANCH SLIME
PROTECTS THESE SEA SLUGS FROM GETTING STUNG BY THE CORALS, JELLYFISH, AND ANEMONES **WHOSE VENOM THEY STEAL** AND **STORE** TO USE ON POTENTIAL PREDATORS.

SOME ANIMALS HAVE SUPERSENSITIVE SNIFFERS ...

I smell SUPPER!

The inside of a GRIZZLY BEAR'S NOSE is 100 TIMES BIGGER than a human's.

The **ALBATROSS CAN SMELL** its fishy, underwater prey from more than **12 MILES** (19 km) **AWAY.**

An **ELEPHANT'S NOSE** can detect water from **12 MILES** (19 km) **AWAY.**

27

...AND SOME ANIMALS CAN
SMELL WITHOUT A NOSE
AT ALL.

MALE MOTHS use their **FEATHERY ANTENNAE** to pick up scents from females that are **MILES AWAY.**

CRABS use a group of **DENSE HAIRS** on their **ANTENNAE** to smell.

SNAKES capture scent particles by **FLICKING THEIR TONGUES** in the air.

BRACHIOSAURUS WAS

HUGE...

Brachiosaurus stood up to **52 FEET** (15.8 m) **TALL,** which is taller than four elephants stacked on top of one another.

From head to tail, it was **80 FEET** (24 m) **LONG**—longer than a tennis court.

Imagine how **BIG** its bones were!

A golden retriever could **FIT INSIDE ITS FOOTPRINT.**

... BUT TITANOSAUR WAS EVEN

BIGGER.

From head to tail, it was **40 FEET** (12 m) **LONGER** than *Brachiosaurus*—that's the length of two orcas!

Titanosaur was at least **15 FEET** (5 m) **LONGER** than the **BLUE WHALE**, the largest animal on Earth today.

It weighed **ONE ELEPHANT MORE** than *Brachiosaurus*.

Its **NECK** alone was almost the **LENGTH OF A SCHOOL BUS.**

YIKES!

STOP

BUS NO. 99

33

BIRDS AREN'T BIRDBRAINS.

CARRION CROWS place nuts in the middle of the road so cars will **CRUSH THE SHELLS** and the crows can retrieve the meat.

A **WOODPECKER FINCH** uses a cactus needle or sharp twig to **DIG INSECTS OUT OF HOLES** and **SPEAR THEM TO DEATH.**

MALE COCKATOOS BEAT TWIGS LIKE DRUMSTICKS against hollow trees to attract females—each cockatoo rhythm is unique.

GREEN HERONS place bait like insects on top of water to **LURE FISH TO THE SURFACE,** and then grab the fish with their beak.

35

LIGHTNING

DOESN'T JUST HAPPEN DURING THUNDERSTORMS.

"DRY" LIGHTNING— WHEN THERE IS LITTLE OR NO ACCOMPANYING RAIN—CAN CAUSE FOREST FIRES.

AN AIRPLANE **FLYING CLOSE** TO A **HEAVILY CHARGED CLOUD** DURING A SNOWSTORM CAN TRIGGER LIGHTNING.

DURING THE 2015 CALBUCO **VOLCANIC ERUPTION** IN CHILE, LIGHTNING FORMED FROM THE INTENSE HEAT GENERATED BY THE MOLTEN LAVA AND GIANT ASH PLUMES.

Benjamin Franklin

LIGHTNING'S SHOCKING HISTORY

Lightning is fascinating ... and sometimes frightening! In the 1750s, scientists—Benjamin Franklin famously among them—demonstrated that lightning is a form of electricity, offering a scientific explanation for the brilliant white zigzags of light that crackled through the sky. But before we had science to tell us exactly what it is and how it's formed, our ancestors had their own ideas. Lightning was described as fire that was captured from the sky to give us warmth. Some ancient cultures believed lightning was a good omen, sent by gods to indicate sacred ground. Greek and Roman temples were often erected at sites where lightning had struck. Similarly, the Navajo Indians believed that lightning had the power to heal people and help crops grow. Other superstitions across many cultures credited certain objects with protection against lightning's power. Acorns from oak trees—which not only remained undamaged but flourished when lightning struck—were placed in windowsills to offer homes the same resilience. Loudly ringing a church bell was also believed to ward off a strike. Today, thanks to Benjamin Franklin, many buildings are fashioned with a tall, narrow lightning rod made of aluminum or copper. The rod redirects the blazing, damaging heat away from the structure and directs it on a safer path toward the ground.

DESPITE THEIR SWEET NAME, **HONEY BADGERS** ARE SURPRISINGLY **TOUGH** AND **FIERCE.**

He took my **HONEY,** too.

THOUGH SMALL, **HONEY BADGERS** OFTEN **WIN FIGHTS WITH LARGE PREDATORS** LIKE LIONS, LEOPARDS, AND HYENAS.

THEY SOMETIMES EAT VENOMOUS SNAKES LIKE COBRAS AND ARE SEEMINGLY **RESISTANT** TO THE **VENOM.**

THEIR **SKIN IS THICK** ENOUGH TO WITHSTAND BEE STINGS, AFRICAN PORCUPINE NEEDLES, SNAKE FANGS, AND LION TEETH.

THEIR **BITE** IS STRONG ENOUGH TO **BREAK A TORTOISE'S SHELL.**

Let's all share the Earth, **OK?**

Threatened ANIMAL SPECIES can recover.

EFFORTS TO **PROTECT WOLVES** HAVE INCREASED THEIR NUMBERS **FROM 300 TO MORE THAN 5,000.**

THE FUR TRADE IN THE EARLY 1900S **REDUCED** THE SEA OTTER POPULATION **TO NEARLY 1,000,** BUT **A CENTURY LATER, THERE ARE MORE THAN 100,000 SEA OTTERS** WORLDWIDE.

THE **PANDA POPULATION GREW 17 PERCENT** IN 10 YEARS, WHICH MOVED PANDAS **OFF THE ENDANGERED LIST.**

THE NUMBER OF **BENGAL TIGERS WAS DOWN TO 120** IN 2009, BUT **HAS ALMOST DOUBLED SINCE.**

43

EARTH CAN BRING THE HEAT.

Lightning can warm the air around it to **50,000°F** (27,760°C), which is **five times hotter** than the surface of the sun.

44

Volcanoes in Hawaii have the hottest lava: up to **2282°F** (1250°C), which is almost **11 times hotter** than the boiling point of water.

SOME ANIMALS CAN LIVE A

LONG TIME...

THE GEODUCK—A GIANT CLAM THAT CAN REACH UP TO **FOUR FEET** (1.2 M) LONG—CAN LIVE **MORE THAN 100 YEARS.**

AFTER FINDING SCARS FROM 19TH-CENTURY WEAPONS ON A **BOWHEAD WHALE,** SCIENTISTS REALIZED THIS ANIMAL—**THE LONGEST-LIVING MAMMAL**—COULD LIVE FOR **UP TO 200 YEARS.**

UNLESS IT GETS SICK OR IS EATEN, THE **"IMMORTAL JELLYFISH" DOES NOT DIE;** AT ANY TIME, IT CAN TRANSFORM BACK TO A POLYP, ITS **EARLIEST STAGE OF LIFE.**

... AND SOME DON'T LIVE

VERY LONG

AT ALL.

MOST **MONARCH BUTTERFLIES** LIVE FOR ONLY **TWO TO SIX WEEKS,** DYING AFTER THEY LAY THEIR EGGS.

A **QUEEN BEE** CAN LIVE UP TO **FIVE YEARS,** BUT HER **WORKER BEES** LIVE **ONLY A FEW WEEKS.**

MAYFLIES SPEND UP TO **TWO YEARS** UNDERWATER IN THE **LARVAL STAGE,** BUT LIVE FOR JUST **ONE DAY** AS FULLY FORMED ADULTS.

SATURN IS THE RINGMASTER OF SPACE . . .

Even with particles and **4,400 POUNDS** (1,996 kg) **OF WATER** raining down from Saturn's rings every second, it will take **100 MILLION** years before the rings **could disappear.**

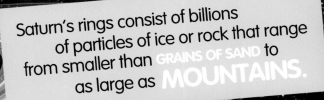

Saturn's rings consist of billions of particles of ice or rock that range from smaller than GRAINS OF SAND to as large as MOUNTAINS.

Saturn's rings span **170,000 MILES** (273,588 km), which equals the distance of almost **SEVEN TRIPS** around Earth.

...AND ITS **MOONS** ARE AS **UNIQUE** AS A CIRCUS ACT.

IAPETUS, known as Saturn's **TWO-FACED MOON,** is white on one side and black on the other.

There is evidence of a **volcano** that explodes **ICE INSTEAD OF LAVA** on Saturn's largest moon, **TITAN.**

Where's my **CLOWN CAR?**

Saturn's moon **ENCELADUS** has an ocean hidden beneath its icy surface that scientists think could **POTENTIALLY HOLD LIFE.**

A NASA image of Kraken Mare's shoreline

SPACE
SUBMARINES

In 2004, NASA discovered a body of liquid on Titan, Saturn's largest moon. Aside from Earth, Titan is the only other celestial body known to have lakes, rivers, and seas on its surface. Yet unlike Earth, the liquid on Titan's surface is made of methane or ethane instead of water. (On Earth, methane is a natural gas that is used as fuel.) The type of life that could exist within this environment could be very different from life as we know it on Earth. Recognizing that this body of liquid likely holds some surprises, NASA named the largest body of liquid Kraken Mare after folklore's legendary sea monster.

To dig deeper into what those surprises might be, NASA is gearing up for an epic space adventure. Getting to Titan won't be easy. It will take years for the spacecraft to reach Titan, and then it has to land safely on the moon's wild surface. The spacecraft will need to be able to submerge itself in Kraken Mare and other liquid bodies on Titan to collect data, all while withstanding Titan's extreme temperatures, dense atmosphere, sporadic weather, and any other potential unknowns. NASA has a big job ahead, but the excitement of what the world's first space submarine could discover is a monster worth tackling.

55

DRAGONS DIFFER AROUND THE WOR

THE DRAGON OF MANY **CHINESE LEGENDS,** OFTEN PICTURED WITHOUT WINGS, WAS CONSIDERED TO BE THE BEARER OF **LUCK AND GOOD FORTUNE.**

THE SNALLYGASTER, A DRAGON-LIKE CREATURE REPORTEDLY SIGHTED IN PARTS OF THE **NORTHEASTERN UNITED STATES,** WAS DESCRIBED AS HALF REPTILE, HALF BIRD WITH RAZOR-SHARP **TEETH USED TO SUCK ITS VICTIMS' BLOOD.**

EVEN **WORLD LEADERS** CAN BE **KIDS AT HEART.**

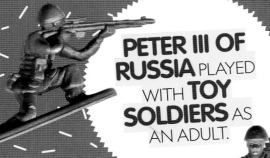

PETER III OF RUSSIA PLAYED WITH **TOY SOLDIERS** AS AN ADULT.

AFTER VISITING FRANCE, **KING LUDWIG II** OF BAVARIA WANTED TO **BUILD "FAIRY-TALE" CASTLES** THROUGHOUT GERMANY.

FRENCH EMPEROR **NAPOLEON BONAPARTE** WAS SAID TO ALWAYS KEEP **LICORICE** IN HIS POCKET.

U.S. PRESIDENT **CALVIN COOLIDGE HID UNDER HIS DESK** TO TRICK HIS BODYGUARDS.

SLIME GIVES SNAILS

SUPERPOWERS.

SLIME HELPS SNAILS **MOVE FASTER,** ESPECIALLY WHEN THEY FIND A SLIME TRAIL **CREATED BY ANOTHER SNAIL.**

WATER SNAILS CAN USE THEIR SLIME TO **WALK UPSIDE DOWN** ON **THE WATER'S SURFACE.**

SLIME ACTS AS **ARMOR, PROTECTING SNAILS** FROM **SHARP OBJECTS** AND **HARMFUL BACTERIA.**

SLIME TIME!

Snails and slugs are part of the gastropod family, a name that comes from two Greek words meaning "stomach" and "foot." This diverse group of animals, found everywhere on Earth, crawls on a single muscular appendage, oozing slime as they move. This slime, or mucus, also offers protection: In dry, hot weather, a land snail uses slime to seal itself in its shell, tucking away from the sun's ultraviolet rays. But the world of gastropods is vast, and some of these creatures have more than just slime to survive a life lived in slow motion. The moon snail uses its seven rows of teeth to drag clams deep into the sand. With a harpoon-like tooth, the geography cone snail delivers a toxic venom strong enough to kill a person. One type of snail—the world's longest—lives as a parasite inside a sea cucumber. And the bright green photosynthetic sea slug, a leaf look-alike and a leaf thief, steals chloroplasts—the parts of a plant that harvest the sun's energy for food—so that it can go without eating algae for nine months or more, feeding off the sun's rays instead.

Photosynthetic sea slug

Ghost stories are global ...

Is it HOWL-OWEEN yet?

The GHOST OF A DRUMMER BOY was said to appear in Edinburgh Castle in Scotland, when the castle was under attack.

At the Valley of the Kings in Egypt, many people have claimed to see the GHOST OF AN EGYPTIAN PHARAOH riding in a fiery chariot with black phantom horses.

At an abandoned hospital in Australia, some say they've heard a YOUNG GIRL'S MUSIC BOX PLAYING just before midnight.

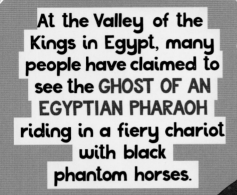

At Eltz Castle, Germany, you might still hear the CLINKING AND CLANKING OF THE KNIGHTS who once protected the castle.

...AND HAVE BEEN AROUND FOR CENTURIES.

Homer, an ancient Greek poet, **wrote about ghosts in the eighth century** B.C.—more than **2,800 years ago!**

Pliny, a Roman author, wrote **2,000 years ago** about the **ghost of an old man in rattling chains** who haunted his house.

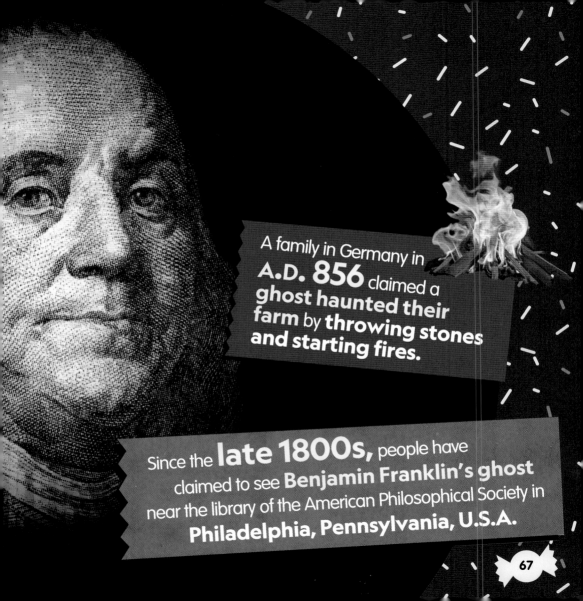

A family in Germany in **A.D. 856** claimed a **ghost haunted their farm** by **throwing stones and starting fires.**

Since the **late 1800s,** people have claimed to see **Benjamin Franklin's ghost** near the library of the American Philosophical Society in **Philadelphia, Pennsylvania, U.S.A.**

BIRDS ARE
MASTER ARCHITECTS.

The **WORLD'S SMALLEST NEST**, **JUST OVER AN INCH** (2.5 cm) **WIDE** and made by the bee hummingbird, is **STRENGTHENED BY SPIDERWEBS**.

SWIFTLET BIRDS use their **SALIVA TO MAKE** their nests.

To keep their eggs warm, **MALLEEFOWL** make a mound out of **HEAT-GENERATING, ROTTING LEAVES** and place the eggs inside.

THE PRAYING MANTIS IS A TRICKSTER.

With its pastel color and petal-like features, the **ORCHID PRAYING MANTIS** often **attracts more bugs than a flower does.**

The
SPINY FLOWER MANTIS
startles attackers by raising its wings—**revealing scary-looking eyespots**—and spreading its arms to look bigger.

The
DEAD LEAF MANTIS looks exactly like the **leaves and branches** where it lives.

SHOW-OFF!

OINK, OINK ... just kidding!

Some animals have MISLEADING NAMES.

THE **FLYING FOX** IS A TYPE OF **BAT**.

THE **FIREFLY** IS A **BEETLE**.

THE **GUINEA PIG** IS A **RODENT**.

THE **MOUNTAIN CHICKEN** IS THE NAME OF A **FROG**.

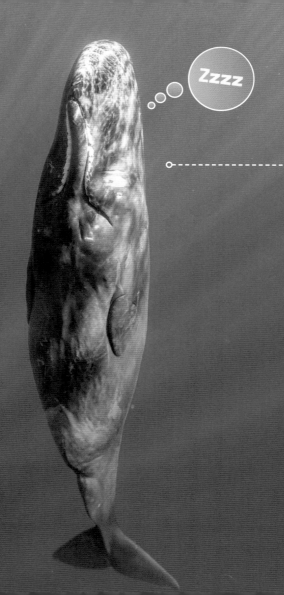

Zzzz

THE **SPERM WHALE** **SLEEPS** **VERTICALLY** WITH ITS HEAD TOWARD THE WATER'S SURFACE, LOOKING AS IF IT IS **STANDING UP ON ITS TAIL.**

THE **BELUGA WHALE CHIRPS.**

THE **SOUTHERN RIGHT WHALE** **LOVES TO** **"SAIL"** — IT STICKS ITS TAIL OUT OF THE WATER TO **CATCH THE WIND.**

NOT **EVERY** ANIMAL **PASSES** GAS . . .

Excuse YOU!

BIRDS DON'T PASS GAS because their **STOMACH LACKS THE BACTERIA** that make gas build up.

Octopuses don't pass gas, but they do **SQUIRT INK!**

Sloths don't pass gas because **THEY DIGEST FOOD TOO SLOWLY** to create it.

... BUT SOME ANIMALS TOOT TO SURVIVE.

Hello!

The tiny herring fish uses **TOOTS TO COMMUNICATE.**

If the bolson pupfish doesn't toot **FREQUENTLY ENOUGH, IT WILL DIE.**

Manatees hold in their toots to **HELP THEM SWIM,** releasing them when they are ready to sink.

LIGHT MOVES **REALLY** FAST. TRAVELING AT THE SPEED OF LIGHT YOU COULD ...

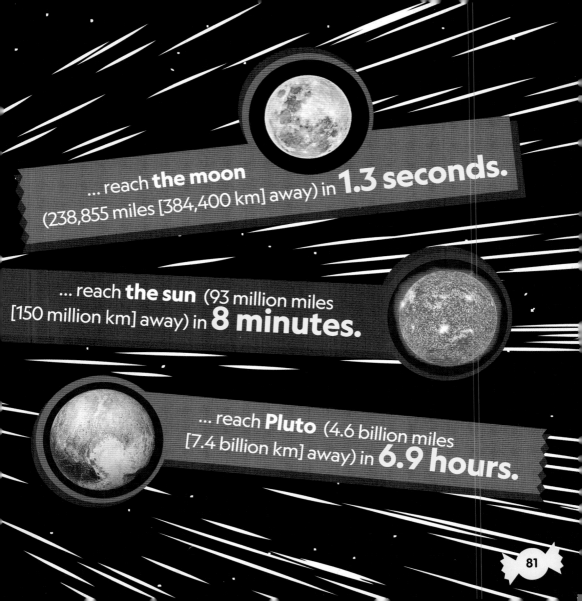

... reach **the moon** (238,855 miles [384,400 km] away) in **1.3 seconds.**

... reach **the sun** (93 million miles [150 million km] away) in **8 minutes.**

... reach **Pluto** (4.6 billion miles [7.4 billion km] away) in **6.9 hours.**

RAIN ISN'T ALWAYS WATER...

In **1894**, **JELLYFISH** **RAINED DOWN** on Bath, England.

SUGAR CRYSTALS SHOWERED Lake County, California, U.S.A., in **1857**.

In **1940**, a tornado scooped up a trove of **16TH-CENTURY COINS**, which then dropped onto Meschera, Russia.

In 2015, millions of **SPIDERS SPEWED FROM THE SKY** in Goulburn, Australia.

...ESPECIALLY ON **OTHER** PLANETS.

Planet HD 189733b, a planet **outside of our solar system,** is bright blue, which scientists think is because of **raining glass.**

Saturn, HERE I COME!

During lightning storms on Saturn, it **rains diamonds.**

Hot acid rains down on Venus, though it becomes a gas before hitting the ground.

ANIMAL BLOOD
COMES IN A RAINBOW
OF COLORS.

Who KNEW?

Some insects have **YELLOW BLOOD**, depending on the **plants they eat.**

Some **SKINKS,** a type of **lizard,** have **GREEN BLOOD.**

The **blood** of **OCELLATED FISH** is completely **CLEAR.**

SQUIDS have **BLUE BLOOD.**

I'm PARCHED!

MAKING **MUMMIES** TOOK **TIME...**

Mummy of Ramses II
circa 1271–1213 B.C.

Wrapping a mummy in bandages—including wrapping **EACH TOE AND FINGER INDIVIDUALLY**—could take **UP TO TWO WEEKS.**

To dry out the body, it was covered inside and out with a special **SALT POWDER** and left for **35 TO 40 DAYS.**

From beginning to end, the **PROCESS TOOK 70 DAYS.**

... AND
RESOURCES.

A replica of
Tutankhamun's tomb

WHILE A BODY WAS DRYING, **A GUARD STOOD BY** TO MAKE SURE **NO ONE, INCLUDING ANIMALS, TOOK IT.**

A **SPECIAL HOOK** WAS USED TO CAREFULLY **REMOVE THE BRAIN** IN SMALL PIECES **THROUGH THE NOSTRILS,** SO AS NOT TO DISFIGURE THE FACE.

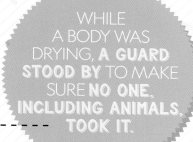

MUMMIES WERE WRAPPED IN **4,000 SQUARE FEET** (372 SQ M) OF BANDAGES, MOST OFTEN COLLECTED FROM OLD CLOTHING OR HOUSEHOLD LINENS.

WHEN THE MUMMY WAS FINISHED, IT WAS PLACED IN A TOMB WITH **FOOD, CLOTHING, AND JEWELRY,** AND SOMETIMES EVEN **BOATS, CHARIOTS, WEAPONS, AND GAMES.**

jewelry

SWEDEN
IS MADE UP OF ABOUT
221,800
ISLANDS.

The capital alone—Stockholm—is made up of **14 ISLANDS.**

If Sweden's population were spread evenly, about **45 PEOPLE** would live on each island.

To visit each island in one year, you'd have to see about **607 ISLANDS A DAY.**

Only **606 MORE** to go!

Wake up!
Time for my
LUNCH!

SOME ANIMALS HAVE UNEXPECTED PARTNERSHIPS.

THE GOBY FISH AND PISTOL SHRIMP BOND AT A YOUNG AGE—THE SHRIMP IS **BLIND** AND USES THE GOBY TO **"SEE,"** WHILE THE SHRIMP BURROWS HOLES TO **PROVIDE A HOME FOR THE GOBY.**

PLOVER BIRDS EAT THE LEECHES OFF **CROCODILES' GUMS.**

THE CARRIER CRAB CARRIES AN **URCHIN** ON ITS BACK TO HELP **PROTECT** IT FROM **PREDATORS.**

BARBEL FISH CLEAN HIPPOS, EATING TICKS AND PARASITES ON THEIR **SKIN** AND **LEFTOVER FOOD** ON THEIR **TEETH.**

EGGS
ARE
EGGSTRAORDINARY
NURSERIES.

THE **PATTERN** OF A JAPANESE QUAIL EGG IS **SPECIFIC TO EACH FEMALE BIRD;** SO TO KEEP THEM SAFE, THESE QUAILS LAY THEIR EGGS IN A SPOT THAT PROVIDES THE BEST CAMOUFLAGE.

THE CHANNELED APPLE SNAIL'S EGGS HAVE TWO DIFFERENT KINDS OF PROTEINS THAT MAKE THEM BOTH **TOXIC AND INDIGESTIBLE** TO PREDATORS.

THE SNOWY OWL'S EGGSHELL PROTECTS THE OWLET FROM **THE SUN,** WHICH SHINES **24 HOURS A DAY** DURING AN ARCTIC SUMMER.

FOR SOME TURTLE AND ALLIGATOR SPECIES, THE **TEMPERATURE OUTSIDE** THE EGGS CAN DETERMINE **THE HATCHLINGS' GENDER.**

FIRE TRUCKS

HAVE CHANGED A LOT OVER THE YEARS.

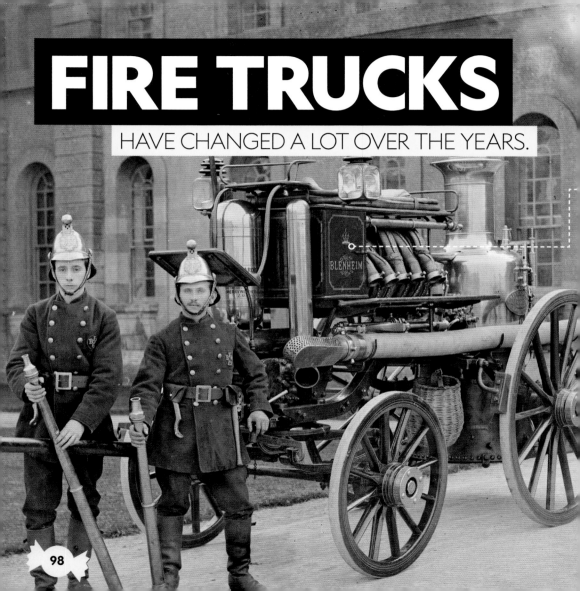

FIRE "TRUCKS" IN **COLONIAL AMERICA** WERE **PEOPLE** WHO WOULD PUT OUT A FIRE WITH AN **ASSEMBLY LINE OF BUCKETS.**

THE **FIRST FIRE TRUCKS** WERE **WATER PUMPS ON WHEELS,** **PULLED BY HUMANS** AND HORSES.

FIRE TRUCKS **DIDN'T HAVE SEATS** INSIDE UNTIL THE **1960s.**

THE **FIRST FIRE PUMP,** CREATED IN **1721,** COULD HOLD **170 GALLONS** (643 L) OF WATER; TODAY'S FIRE TRUCKS CAN HOLD UP TO **4,000 GALLONS** (15,142 L).

SOME ANIMALS LIKE THEIR PRIVACY ...

HEARD ISLAND, located in the middle of the ocean between Australia and Antarctica, is home to large populations of animals, and **NO ONE IS ALLOWED TO VISIT WITHOUT A PERMIT.**

Did you **HEAR** that?

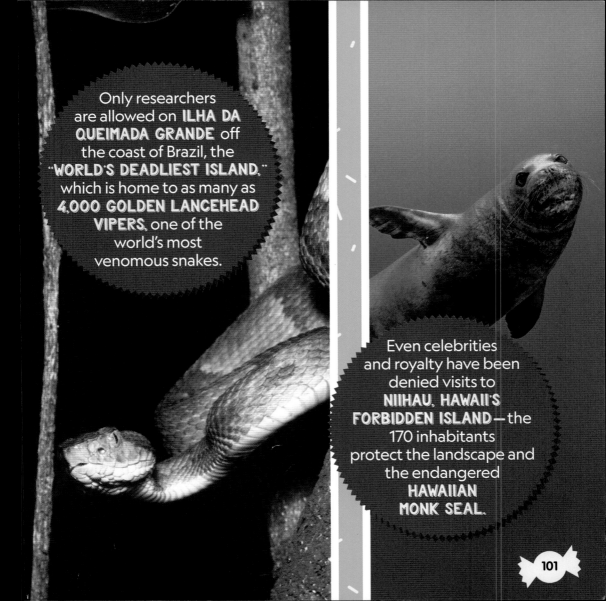

Only researchers are allowed on **ILHA DA QUEIMADA GRANDE** off the coast of Brazil, the "**WORLD'S DEADLIEST ISLAND**," which is home to as many as **4,000 GOLDEN LANCEHEAD VIPERS**, one of the world's most venomous snakes.

Even celebrities and royalty have been denied visits to **NIIHAU, HAWAII'S FORBIDDEN ISLAND**—the 170 inhabitants protect the landscape and the endangered **HAWAIIAN MONK SEAL**.

101

...AND SO DO SOME
SECRET RECIPES.

THE KRISPY KREME doughnut recipe is **KEPT IN A SAFE** at the main plant in Winston-Salem, North Carolina, U.S.A.

It took **MILTON HERSHEY** years to perfect his **HEAVILY GUARDED** milk chocolate recipe and process, dubbed the "**HERSHEY PROCESS.**"

This trick WORKED last time ...

THE WORLD OF COCA-COLA in Atlanta, Georgia, U.S.A. has a **VAULT** that secures the secret recipe to the beverage—**NO ONE IS ALLOWED** inside.

103

WHAT?
Table manners just aren't my thing.

HOUSEFLIES CAN BE DISGUSTING...

Houseflies **TASTE WITH THEIR FEET**, which is why they like to land on our food.

Houseflies like to **EAT POOP AND GARBAGE**, and they lay eggs on them too.

POOP ZONE

LACKING TEETH, houseflies use a mixture of their **SALIVA** and **REGURGITATED FOOD** to liquefy their meal—then they **SLURP** it down.

A housefly produces more than **100 EGGS** at a time, which can hatch within **12 TO 24 HOURS**.

... AND
DANGEROUS.

Before the invention of **antibiotic** medicines, **flies** were considered **deadly.**

A **single housefly** can carry more than **one million** bacteria.

Houseflies can **transmit** up to **65 different diseases** to **humans.**

During the **Spanish-American War in 1898,** more **soldiers died** from disease **spread by flies** than from **battle wounds.**

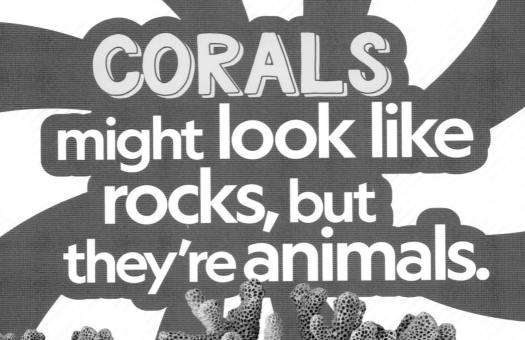

CORALS might look like **look like** rocks, but they're animals.

THEY ARE **RELATED TO JELLYFISH** AND **SEA ANEMONES.**

A CORAL IS A **POLYP,** A TINY ORGANISM THAT **ATTACHES TO A ROCK** AND BUDS MORE POLYPS, EVENTUALLY **CONNECTING WITH OTHER CORALS TO MAKE A REEF.**

THEY ARE AMONG THE OLDEST ANIMALS; SOME BEGAN GROWING **50 MILLION YEARS AGO.**

CORALS HAVE A MOUTH ENCIRCLED BY **VENOMOUS TENTACLES.**

LAKES CONTAIN SECRETS BENEATH THEIR SURFACE.

In 2016, a boater claimed to have discovered a deep crevice in Loch Ness Lake in Scotland, **A POTENTIAL NEW PLACE** to search for the Loch Ness **MONSTER**.

For most of the year, Green Lake in Austria is a park, but in June, water levels triple, creating a lake with **UNDERWATER BENCHES, BRIDGES, HIKING TRAILS,** and **LEAFY TREES.**

In 2011, a drought in Texas, U.S.A., caused lakes across the state to dry up, **REVEALING A PREHISTORIC SKULL, ANCIENT TOOLS, TOMBSTONES,** and even an old baseball field.

SOME ANIMALS **FEED** THEIR YOUNG IN **PECULIAR** WAYS.

A DESERT SPIDER **LIQUEFIES ITS OWN ORGANS, VOMITS THEM INTO HER BABIES' MOUTHS,** AND DIES TWO WEEKS LATER.

PLATYPUSES **SWEAT MILK THROUGH THEIR STOMACH** TO FEED THEIR YOUNG.

I'd do anything for my CHILD!

UNTIL THEY ARE A FEW WEEKS OLD, THE LARVAE OF CAECILIANS—WORMLIKE AMPHIBIANS— **TEAR OFF** AND **EAT THEIR MOTHER'S FLESH,** WHICH REGROWS EVERY THREE DAYS.

SNOWFLAKES
ARE SNOW JOKE!

Anyone up for a **SNOWBALL** fight?

It's **extremely rare** to find
TWO IDENTICAL SNOWFLAKES.

The **largest snowflake** ever recorded was **15 INCHES** (38 cm) **WIDE** and **8 INCHES** (20 cm) **THICK—** that's larger than a Frisbee!

Snowflakes **look white,** but they are **ACTUALLY TRANSLUCENT.**

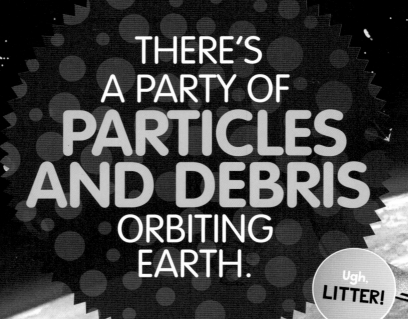

THERE'S A PARTY OF **PARTICLES AND DEBRIS** ORBITING EARTH.

Ugh, LITTER!

There are **20,000** pieces of debris **larger than a softball** orbiting Earth.

There are **500,000** pieces of debris **larger than a marble** orbiting Earth.

There are **millions of particles** orbiting Earth that are **too small to track.**

Particles orbit Earth **nearly 17 times in one day** at speeds up to **17,500 miles an hour** (28,164 km/h).

LET'S GO FISHING ...
IN SPACE!

Hundreds of thousands of pieces of "space junk"—ranging from tiny flecks of spacecraft paint to large satellites no longer in use—orbit Earth at a speedy 17,500 miles an hour (28,164 km/h). While "pollution" in space might not sound like trouble—after all, who could it bother?—human-made space debris has become a growing problem since the late 1950s. Scientists are watching about 20,000 specific pieces to make sure they don't slam into each other and explode into even more space shrapnel that could potentially harm a spacecraft. The International Space Station can be severely damaged by just a fleck of paint orbiting at breakneck speed, and it sometimes has to maneuver out of the way if a larger piece is hurtling toward it. The more spacecraft we send up, the more space junk there will be, so scientists are figuring out ways to corral it. They are working to develop nets that can capture debris, harpoons that can spear objects, and sails that could slow down fast-moving pieces. All these methods would drag the debris down to Earth's atmosphere, where it would burn up. Space isn't just an endless sea of stars and planets with plenty of room to spare; we need to keep it clean so our astronauts stay safe and so we can explore and discover amazing new phenomena.

New technologies are being built to clean up space.

PUMPKINS SET PREPOSTEROUS RECORDS!

A man **SMASHED** a record **31 PUMPKINS** in **ONE MINUTE** with a **HAMMER**.

The world's **LARGEST PUMPKIN** weighed **2,624 POUNDS** (1,190 KG)—that's as big as a **SMALL CAR**.

WOW! Can I have some?

The world's **LARGEST PUMPKIN PIE** weighed **3,699 POUNDS** (1,678 KG)—that's heavier than a **WALRUS**.

CRYSTALS ARE
EXTRAORDINARY.

Tightly squeezing a **quartz crystal** can **create** an **electric current.**

Vikings used a crystal called **Iceland spar to help** them find the sun and **navigate** their ships on cloudy days.

The **crystal galena** can **extract music and voices** from **radio waves.**

If you **smash a sugar cube** with the bottom of a glass in a pitch-black room, **a faint blue glow will appear** as the sugar crystals break apart.

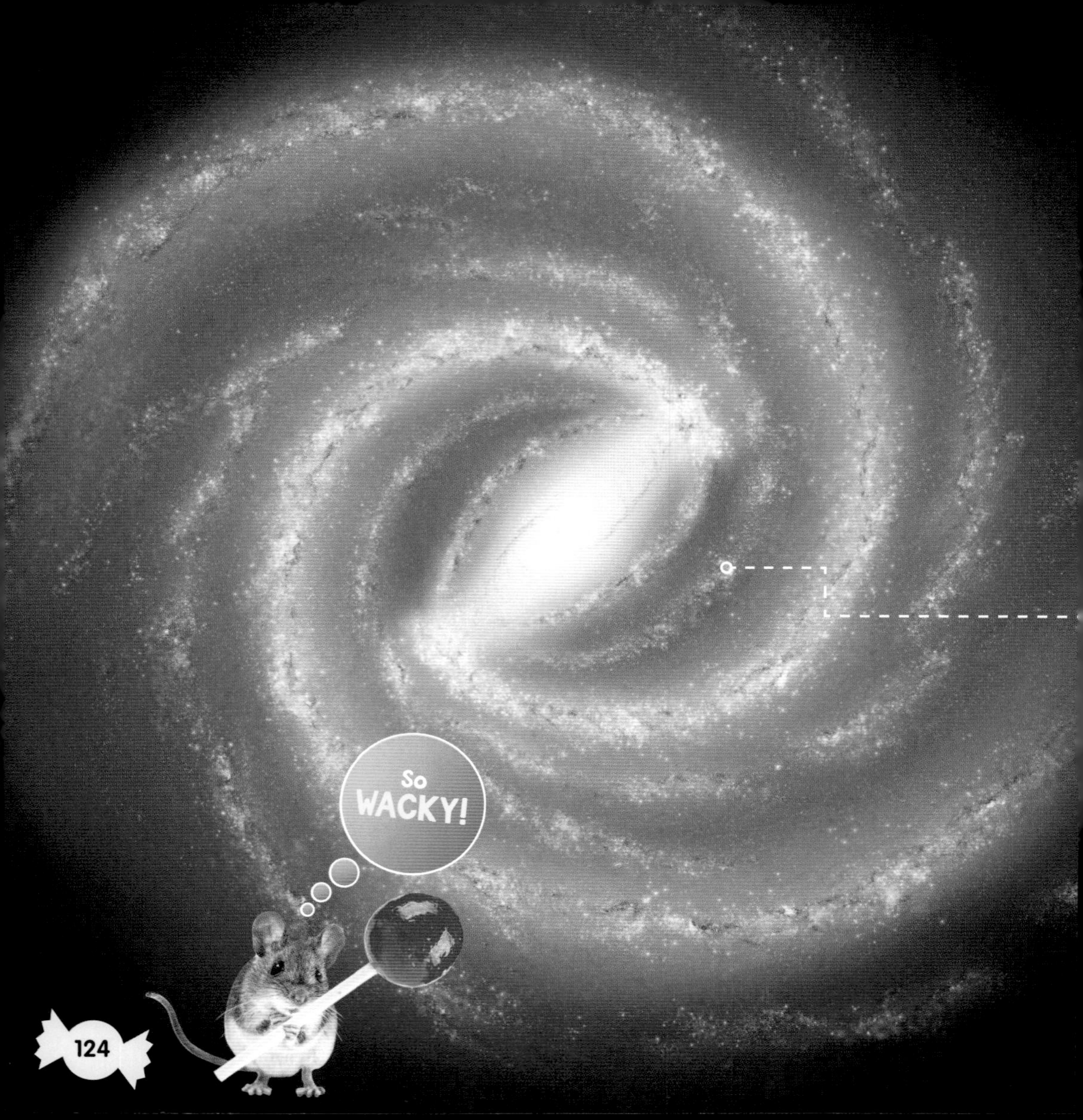
So
WACKY!

NATURE IS FULL OF SPIRALS.

"SNOW ROLLERS" ARE CREATED WHEN WIND ROLLS SNOW INTO A HOLLOW SPIRAL THAT LOOKS LIKE **A DOUGHNUT.**

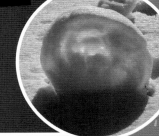

ABOUT **72 PERCENT** OF THE GALAXIES SCIENTISTS HAVE DISCOVERED ARE **SPIRAL GALAXIES,** INCLUDING OUR OWN GALAXY, **THE MILKY WAY.**

BLIND ARMY ANTS USE SMELL TO FOLLOW THE LEADER ANT, BUT IF THE LEADER VEERS OFF COURSE, THE ANTS WILL FOLLOW EACH OTHER **IN A SPIRAL.**

125

FOOTPRINTS DON'T ALWAYS DISAPPEAR.

THE OLDEST **HUMAN FOOTPRINT** IN NORTH AMERICA IS FROM **13,000** YEARS AGO.

THE OLDEST **FOOTPRINTS** DISCOVERED ON EARTH ARE **541 MILLION** YEARS OLD AND MOST LIKELY BELONG TO AN EARLY INSECT.

THE FIRST FOOTPRINT ON **THE MOON** WILL REMAIN FOR AT LEAST **A MILLION YEARS**— THERE'S NO WIND TO BLOW IT AWAY.

Practice makes PERFECT!

SOUTH KOREA IS HOME TO **110-MILLION-YEAR-OLD** FOOTPRINTS THAT SHOW THE FIRST SIGN OF A LIZARD RUNNING ON TWO FEET INSTEAD OF FOUR.

Just don't ask me to play **FETCH!**

DOGS AREN'T THE **ONLY ANIMALS** THAT LIKE TO **EAT BONES.**

GIRAFFES CHEW ON THE BONES OF BUFFALO AND OTHER ANIMALS TO GET THE NUTRIENTS THEY NEED TO **STRENGTHEN THEIR OWN BONES.**

ZOMBIE WORMS CONSUME THE BONES OF **DEAD WHALES** FOR ENERGY.

TO GET THE NUTRIENTS THEY NEED TO KEEP THEIR SHELLS HEALTHY, **LEOPARD TORTOISES** OCCASIONALLY EAT HYENA POOP, WHICH IS FILLED WITH **CHEWED-UP ANIMAL BONES.**

THE TOOTH FAIRY HAS COMPETITORS AROUND THE GLOBE.

IN ARGENTINA,

WHEN A BABY TOOTH IS PLACED IN A CUP OF WATER,

A MOUSE

COMES AND REMOVES THE TOOTH, DRINKS THE WATER, AND **LEAVES A GIFT IN THE EMPTY GLASS.**

IN KOREA, CHILDREN THROW THEIR BABY TOOTH ON THE

ROOF OF THEIR HOUSES

IN HOPES THAT A BLACKBIRD WILL BRING THEM A NEW ONE.

SOME **FOODS** ARE THOUGHT TO BRING **GOOD LUCK.**

Carp is eaten in many **central European** countries on Christmas Eve, and some people carry the **scales in their wallet** for luck.

In many regions of **Greece** on New Year's Eve, people **smash a pomegranate—**. the more seeds that spill out, the luckier you might be that year.

Kit Kats are often eaten in Japan for good luck because the candy's name sounds like the Japanese phrase **kitto katsu,** which means "You surely will win!"

The **plastic baby** inside a **Mardi Gras king cake** is said to **bestow good luck** on the finder.

TORNADOES ON EARTH ARE

POWERFUL...

He
SURVIVED!

A **tornado** in Missouri, U.S.A., **carried a person** farther than the length of **five 747 airplanes** placed end to end.

The widest tornado ever recorded was **2.6 miles (4.2 km) wide**—that's more than 45 American **football fields!**

A tornado's wind speed can reach almost **300 miles an hour** (483 km/h)—that's one and a half times faster than a NASCAR race car.

...BUT **TORNADOES** ON THE SUN ARE EVEN **STRONGER.**

A tornado on the sun can be **124,000 MILES (199,559 KM) HIGH**— big enough to capture **ONE HUNDRED EARTHS** in its spin.

Tornado speeds on the sun can reach **186,000 miles** an hour (300,000 km/h)— **620 TIMES FASTER** than tornado speeds on Earth.

A tornado eruption on the sun **CAN DAMAGE POWER AND COMMUNICATION NETWORKS** on Earth.

WOW!

137

There are more than THREE TRILLION TREES on Earth.

THAT'S ROUGHLY **400 TREES PER PERSON** ON EARTH.

THAT'S **15,236 TREES PER SQUARE MILE** (5,883/SQ KM) OF EARTH'S LAND IF EVENLY DISTRIBUTED.

THAT'S AT LEAST **SEVEN AND A HALF TIMES MORE** THAN THE **NUMBER OF STARS IN THE MILKY WAY.**

So many **HOMES** to choose from!

139

SHARKS HAVE A LOT OF TEETH.

A shark can **LOSE A TOOTH** and **REPLACE IT IN ONE DAY.**

The **FRILLED SHARK** has **300 TEETH** compared to a human's **32 TEETH.**

Most sharks have **FIVE ROWS OF TEETH.** but some sharks have up to **110 ROWS.**

Some sharks have more than **50,000 TEETH IN ONE LIFETIME.**

141

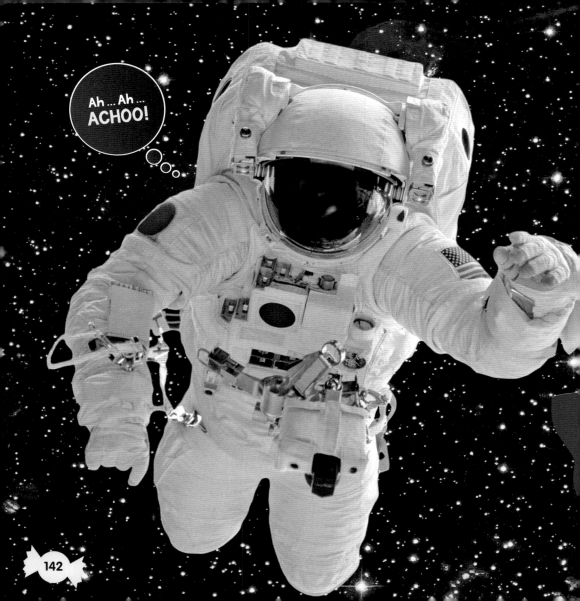

SPACE CAN WREAK HAVOC ON THE HUMAN BODY.

Astronaut Harrison Schmitt is **ALLERGIC TO MOONDUST**— but didn't find that out until he was on the moon.

Without gravity, **HUMAN BONES LOSE DENSITY** at a rate of one percent a month compared to one percent a year on Earth.

COLDS ARE MORE CONTAGIOUS in space because without gravity, infectious particles don't fall to the ground as they do on Earth—they float.

CHOCOLATE

HAS AN ANCIENT PAST...

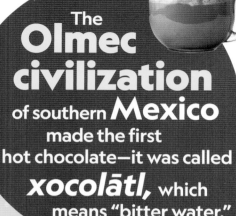

The **Olmec civilization** of southern **Mexico** made the first hot chocolate—it was called *xocolātl,* which means "bitter water."

Maya hot chocolate wasn't sweet—it was often flavored with **chili peppers** instead of sugar.

The cacao bean and the drink it produced were so prized by the **Maya and Aztec** that the beans were used as a **form of currency.**

145

...AND HAS BEEN USED AS **MEDICINE** FOR HUNDREDS OF YEARS.

Eat one **CHOCOLATE BAR** and call me in the morning.

In the **16th century,** hot chocolate was believed to help **cure kidney disease.**

In **17th-century** Florence, some doctors recommended chocolate for a **gassy stomach.**

During the **Revolutionary War,** cacao beans were given to soldiers to boost their energy, and hot chocolate was **given to wounded** soldiers for a quicker recovery.

During **World Wars I and II,** volunteers set up hot chocolate stations near battlefields **for the troops.**

147

EACH **PRESIDENT** ADDED HIS OWN SPECIAL TOUCH TO THE WHITE HOUSE.

Theodore Roosevelt officially gave the White House its name in 1901—previous names included the Executive Mansion, the President's House, and the President's Palace.

Benjamin Harrison installed electricity in the White House, and he was the first president to have a **Christmas tree** there.

Millard Fillmore was the first president to have a **bathtub** with running water installed in the White House.

ANIMAL BARFING CAN BE BIZARRE.

OWLS often **REGURGITATE A PELLET** that contains the entire skeleton of an animal they've eaten because they can't digest the bones.

When threatened, the **WHITE BUTTERFLY CATERPILLAR VOMITS A GREEN FLUID** made of semidigested cabbage that smells and tastes bad to predators.

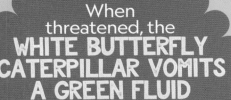

When threatened, a **TURKEY VULTURE VOMITS ITS STINKY INSIDES—** which are acidic enough to burn— on a predator.

BEES swallow flower nectar and store it in a special sac in their abdomen that mixes the nectar with an enzyme, and **IT COMES BACK UP AS HONEY.**

SNOWBALL FIGHTS HAVE MADE

HISTORY.

DURING THE **REVOLUTIONARY WAR,** **GEORGE WASHINGTON** BROKE UP A SNOWBALL FIGHT AMONG SOLDIERS AT HARVARD YARD.

A FRIENDLY SNOWBALL BATTLE BROKE OUT AMONG MORE THAN **9,000 CONFEDERATE SOLDIERS** DURING THE **CIVIL WAR.**

SCORE!

A SNOWBALL FIGHT MIGHT HAVE **STARTED A BATTLE** BETWEEN THE AMERICAN COLONISTS AND BRITISH SOLDIERS ON **MARCH 5, 1770.**

NOT ALL VOLCANOES ARE CREATED EQUAL.

Io, one of Jupiter's moons, is the most volcanically active object in our solar system, with hundreds of volcanoes erupting **lava nearly 100 degrees hotter** than lava on Earth.

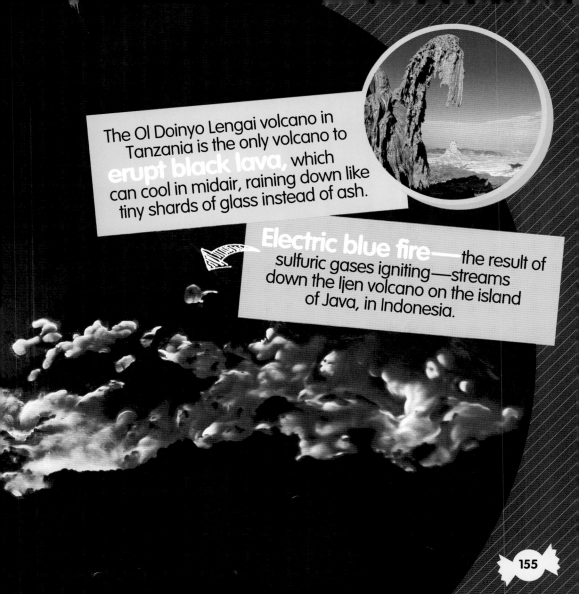

The Ol Doinyo Lengai volcano in Tanzania is the only volcano to **erupt black lava,** which can cool in midair, raining down like tiny shards of glass instead of ash.

Electric blue fire—the result of sulfuric gases igniting—streams down the Ijen volcano on the island of Java, in Indonesia.

155

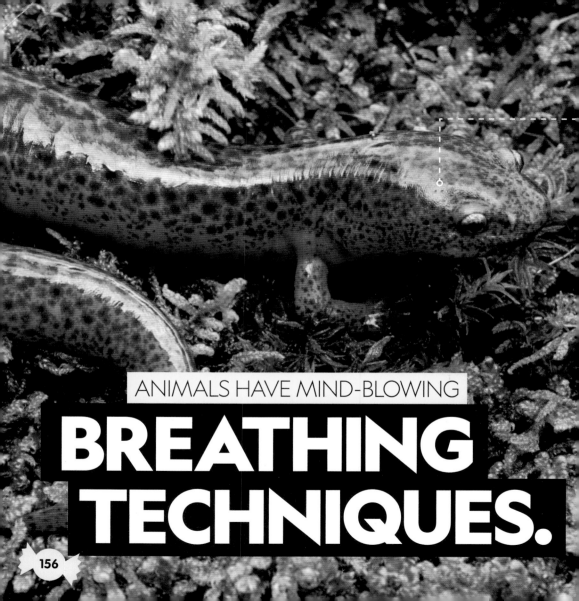

ANIMALS HAVE MIND-BLOWING

BREATHING TECHNIQUES.

SOME **SALAMANDERS** ABSORB OXYGEN **THROUGH THEIR SKIN** AND **THE ROOF OF THEIR MOUTHS.**

THE **DIVING BELL SPIDER** CAN STAY UNDERWATER FOR **24 HOURS** BECAUSE OF **AIR BUBBLES** THAT ATTACH TO ITS **CHEST HAIRS.**

YOUNG **FITZROY RIVER TURTLES** HAVE LUNGS, BUT A SPECIAL LINING IN THEIR BACKSIDE HELPS THEM **ABSORB OXYGEN** SO THAT THEY CAN STAY UNDERWATER FOR UP TO **72 HOURS.**

IN ONE SECOND, A REINDEER'S NOSE WARMS THE COLD AIR BY **70 TO 80°F** (39 TO 44°C) BEFORE THE AIR REACHES ITS LUNGS.

THE SIMPLEST BODILY REACTIONS HAVE THE MOST COMPLICATED NAMES.

Sternutation = **SNEEZING**

Sphenopalatine ganglioneuralgia = **BRAIN FREEZE**

Deglutition = **SWALLOWING**

Horripilation = **GOOSE BUMPS**

Some animals need A LOT OF FOOD to survive ...

BATS CAN EAT **1,000 MOSQUITOES** IN AN HOUR.

NORTH AMERICA'S TINIEST MAMMAL, **THE PYGMY SHREW, HAS TO EAT CONSTANTLY** TO SURVIVE—**ONE HOUR WITHOUT FOOD COULD KILL IT.**

THE **BLUE WHALE** CAN EAT **8,000 POUNDS** (3,629 KG) OF KRILL A DAY—THAT'S LIKE YOU EATING **32,000 CHEESEBURGERS!**

AN **AFRICAN ELEPHANT** NEEDS MORE THAN **70,000 CALORIES** A DAY, WHICH IS ABOUT **30 TIMES MORE** THAN WHAT AN ADULT MALE HUMAN NEEDS.

161

THE MALE **EMPEROR PENGUIN** CAN GO FOR **TWO TO FOUR MONTHS** WITHOUT FOOD, LIVING OFF ITS **LAYER OF FAT.**

...and some need VERY little.

SHARKS CAN **GO SEVERAL WEEKS** WITHOUT EATING, AND THE LONGER THEY DON'T EAT, THE SHARPER THEIR **HUNTING SKILLS** BECOME.

THE HUMP ON A **CAMEL'S BACK** IS STORED FAT THAT HELPS THEM GO FOR **SEVERAL MONTHS** WITHOUT EATING.

CROCODILES CAN LIVE OFF THEIR OWN TISSUE FOR UP TO **THREE YEARS**.

MERMAID
LEGENDS

ARE GLOBAL.

THE **JAPANESE** VERSION OF A MERMAID, **NINGYO,** IS OFTEN SAID TO HAVE HORNS AND POINTY TEETH.

FIN-TASTIC!

MAMI WATA IS A MERMAID-LIKE **AFRICAN** WATER SPIRIT THAT IS KNOWN AS A SNAKE CHARMER.

SELKIES OF **SCOTTISH** LEGEND ARE SEAL-LIKE CREATURES THAT TURN INTO BEAUTIFUL MAIDENS.

TREES CAN TAKE US BY
SURPRISE.

By looking at the **GROWTH RINGS** of a **BRISTLECONE PINE TREE**, scientists can trace weather patterns, volcanic eruptions, and even civilization timelines over the last **9,000 YEARS.**

DRAGON'S BLOOD TREES in Socotra Archipelago, Yemen, get their name from the **RED SAP** that **OOZES FROM THEIR TRUNKS.**

The bark of the **RAINBOW EUCALYPTUS TREE CHANGES COLOR** as layers fall off, making its trunk look like a **RAINBOW.**

FAIRY-TALE
FOREST

The Black Forest in Germany, named for its dense trees that block out the sunlight, is the perfect, enchanting environment for brewing magical stories. According to legend, this forested mountain range inspired some of the Grimm brothers' beloved fairy tales: "Rapunzel," "Sleeping Beauty," "Snow White," and "Hansel and Gretel." Walking on fern-covered footpaths beneath a canopy of pines and firs, you might feel as though you could stumble upon the home of a hidden princess. Strolling past one of the Black Forest's natural hot springs, where for thousands of years people have soaked in the relaxing waters, you might wonder if you too will sleep for a hundred years. But not to worry, the sound of cuckoo clocks, hand-carved for centuries by Black Forest craftsmen, will keep you awake long enough to visit the large castles and small villages nestled among the evergreens.

Hey! Stay AWAKE!

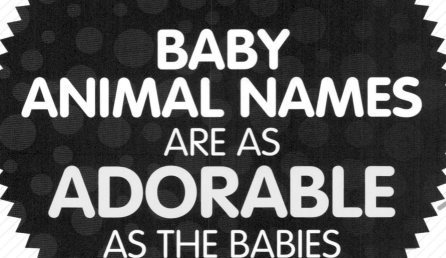

BABY ANIMAL NAMES ARE AS ADORABLE AS THE BABIES THEMSELVES.

Baby dove = **squeaker**

Baby puffin = **puffling**

Baby frog = **pollywog**

Baby fish = **fry**

Baby mouse = **pinky**

YOUR FAVORITE **BASKETBALL TEAM** WAS ALMOST GIVEN A DIFFERENT NAME.

THE BOSTON **UNICORNS** WAS A NAME CONSIDERED FOR THE **BOSTON CELTICS.**

THE **CLEVELAND CAVALIERS** WERE ALMOST CALLED THE CLEVELAND **PRESIDENTS—** SINCE MANY FORMER U.S. PRESIDENTS WERE BORN IN **OHIO.**

THE **ORLANDO MAGIC** WERE ALMOST NAMED THE ORLANDO **JUICE** AFTER FLORIDA'S STATE FRUIT, THE ORANGE.

PRESIDENT **CALVIN COOLIDGE** HAD SOME **WILD PETS.**

HE HAD A **PYGMY HIPPOPOTAMUS** WHOSE FULL NAME WAS **WILLIAM JOHNSON HIPPOPOTAMUS.**

HIS WIFE, GRACE, BUILT A TREE HOUSE FOR **REBECCA, THEIR RACCOON.**

HE ACQUIRED **TWO LION CUBS** FROM JOHANNESBURG, SOUTH AFRICA, NAMED **TAX REDUCTION** AND **BUDGET BUREAU.**

A **FULL MOON** AFFECTS PLANTS AND ANIMALS IN **WEIRD WAYS.**

Corals **reproduce** only once a year, during a full moon.

Antlion larvae, which **dig funnel-shaped holes to catch prey, dig bigger holes** during full moons.

The **wereplant,** named after the mythical werewolf, only **releases its pollen** during a full moon.

SEA CUCUMBERS EAT WITH **THEIR FEET.**

UNLIKE OTHER SPIDERS, **TARANTULAS** CAN **PRODUCE WEBS FROM THEIR FEET** THAT HELP THEM **HANG ON TO SURFACES.**

A PLATYPUS STABS A PREDATOR WITH THE POINTY, **CLAWLIKE SPURS** ON ITS REAR FEET TO INJECT A **PARALYZING VENOM.**

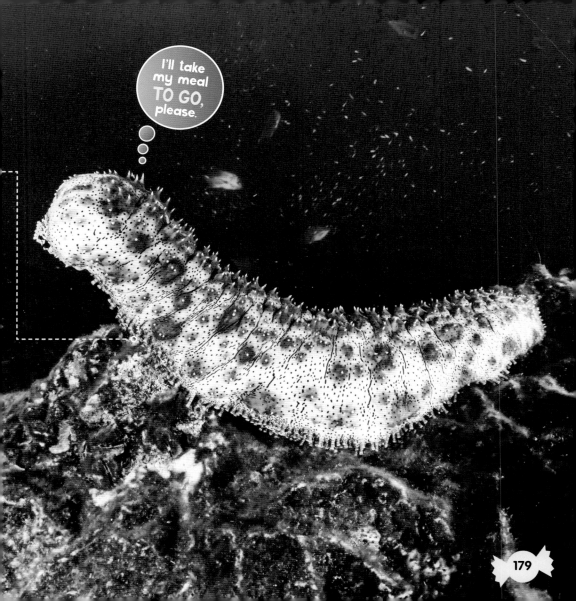

PEOPLE HAVE GONE NUTS FOR DOUGHNUTS FOR HUNDREDS OF YEARS.

Doughnuts—dough balls with **FRUIT**, not a hole, in the center—were called **OLYKOEKS**, or **"OILY CAKES,"** in the mid-19th century by their Dutch creators.

The first **WRITTEN RECORD** of the word "doughnut" was in **1809**—more than 200 years ago!

The **FIRST DOUGHNUTS** were **FRIED IN PORK FAT.**

Archaeologists have found **FOSSILIZED BITS** of what look like doughnuts in **PREHISTORIC NATIVE AMERICAN SETTLEMENTS.**

Get 'em while they're HOT!

A Red Cross member serves doughnuts during WWII.

A SALUTE TO
DOUGHNUTS

Today our calendars are peppered with days celebrating many different kinds of food, from chocolate and ice cream to popcorn and peanut butter. But some national food days are a bit more significant than others. Look to the first Friday of June—National Doughnut Day—when these fried ring-shaped treats with indulgent fillings, colorful sprinkles, and creative toppings steal the sugary spotlight. The Salvation Army created this celebration of the delectable doughnut in 1938 to honor the women who volunteered with the Salvation Army, serving soldiers doughnuts on the front lines during World War I. Two women—so-called "dough lassies"— fried up as many as 2,500 dough-nuts in one day, using shell casings and bottles as rolling pins, empty cans as cookie cutters, and helmets as frying pans. This wartime tradition continued in World War II with the Red Cross and their "doughnut dollies." Doughnuts were said to bring a big boost to soldiers' morale—a sugar high that elevated this humble pastry to a noble cause.

Helpings of doughnuts for WWII soldiers

The world's **STRONGEST** man can lift **1,102 POUNDS, 4.9 OUNCES** (500 kg). That's more than about ...

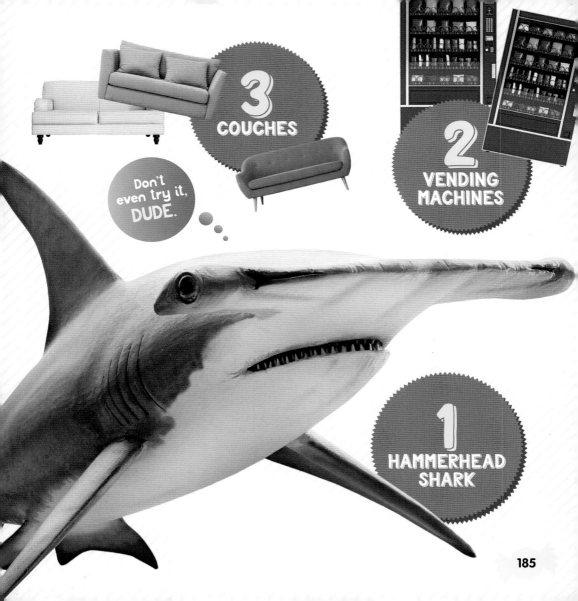

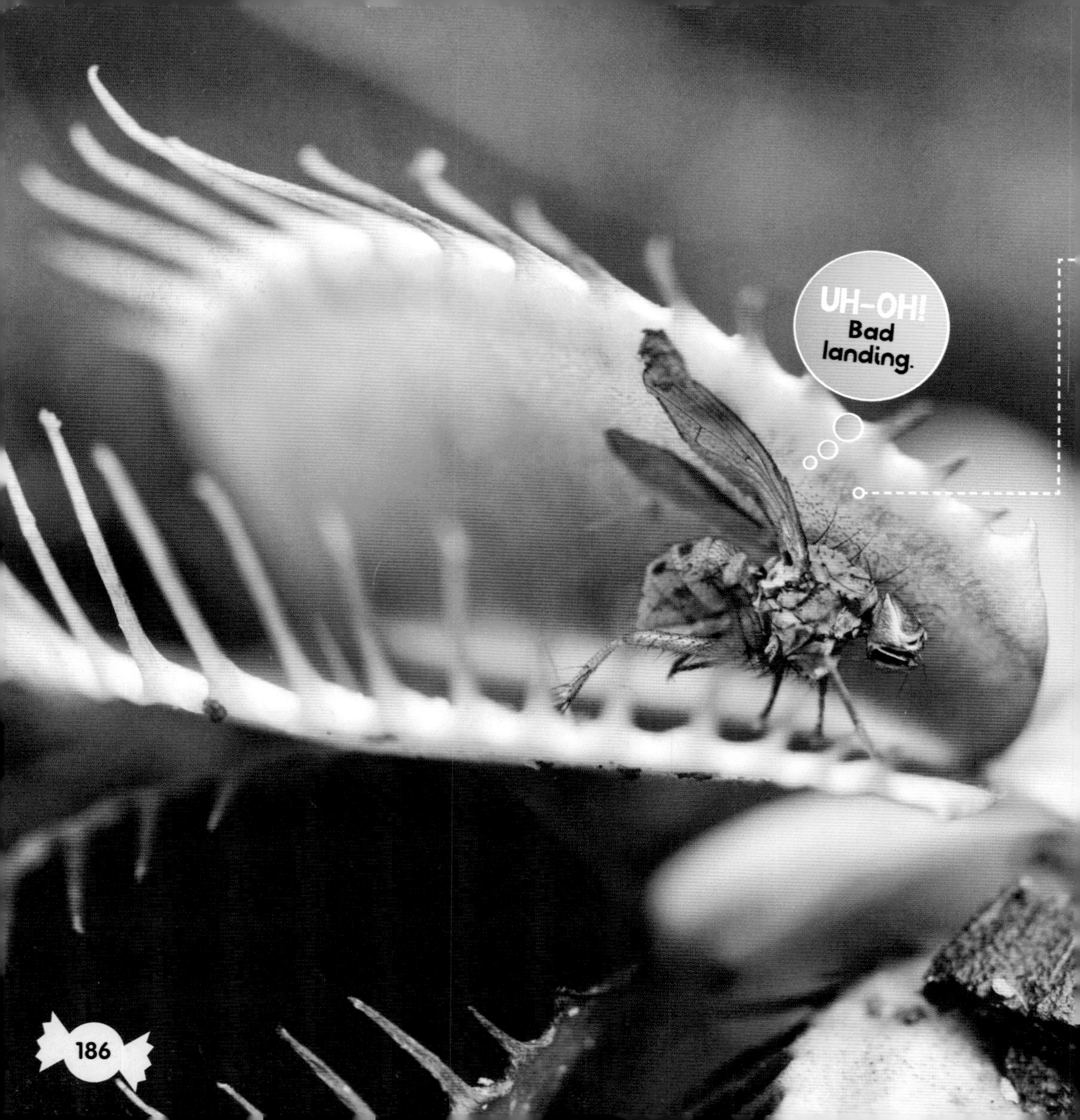
UH-OH!
Bad landing.

WHEN AN INSECT TOUCHES THE **TRIGGER HAIRS** ON A **VENUS FLYTRAP,** THE PLANT'S HINGED LEAVES **SNAP SHUT,** TRAPPING ITS PREY.

THE **PITCHER PLANT** HAS A COLORFUL PITCHER-LIKE OPENING THAT ATTRACTS **CURIOUS INSECTS—** THEY SLIP DOWN ITS WET RIM AND **BECOME PREY.**

SPACECRAFT UNLOCK THE SECRETS OF SPACE.

With the **KEPLER SPACECRAFT,** scientists discovered **2,681 planets** that exist **OUTSIDE OUR SOLAR SYSTEM.**

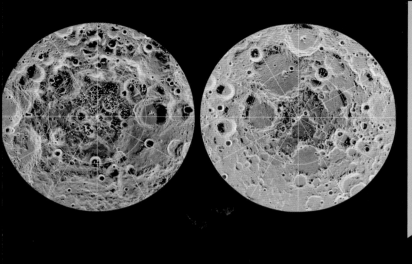

A spacecraft confirmed that there is **ice on Earth's moon,** a possible future resource for rocket fuel or filtered water and oxygen for astronauts.

In 2018, photographs from the **GAIA SPACECRAFT** helped create the **LARGEST STAR MAP** to date—it is **700 million times larger** than the 2016 map.

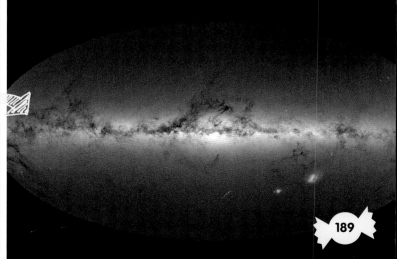

BUGS ARE EATEN AROUND THE GLOBE.

Yum! Tastes like MINT!

Traditional **Brazilian dishes** can include **big, fat ants** called queen ants.

Ant eggs are a favorite dish in **Thailand.**

Wasp larvae are eaten in some parts of **Japan,** often mixed with rice.

In **Ghana, termites** are a source of protein for people, who often roast or fry them.

LITERALLY!

THE GAME OF BASKETBALL HASN'T CHANGED MUCH, BUT THE BALL AND THE BASKET HAVE.

The first games used **peach baskets**— a goal was made when **the ball stayed in the basket.**

The peach basket had a **bottom,** so a person had to **retrieve the ball** each time a basket was made and **put it back into play.**

The **first basketball** was a **soccer ball.**

More than **50 years** after the first game in 1891, an **orange-colored ball** was introduced because it was easier for the **players and spectators** to see.

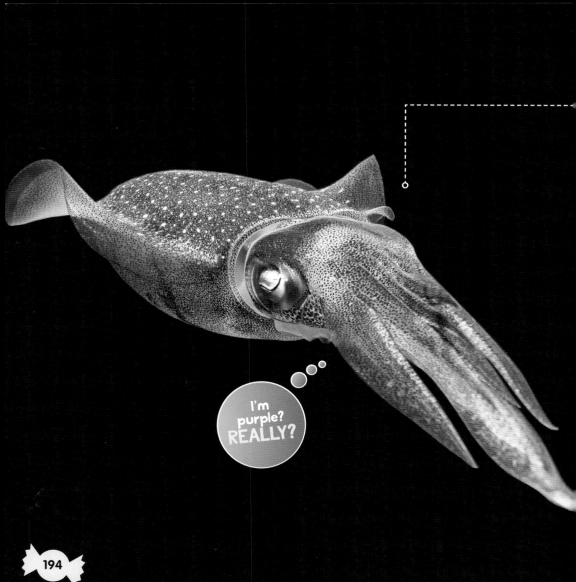

I'm purple? REALLY?

NOT EVERY CREATURE SEES THE SAME COLORS.

SQUID AND OCTOPUSES SEE ONLY IN **BLACK-AND-WHITE.**

THE BLUEBOTTLE BUTTERFLY HAS **FIVE TIMES MORE** PHOTORECEPTORS THAN HUMANS AND SEES MANY MORE COLORS.

Those are some **HOWLIN'** good tunes!

196

THE WORLD'S LONGEST SONG EVER RELEASED IS **13** HOURS, **23** MINUTES, **32** SECONDS LONG.

THE WORLD'S LONGEST CONCERT—PLAYED BY AN **AUTOMATED ORGAN**—WON'T FINISH UNTIL **2640,** LASTING A TOTAL OF **639 YEARS.**

EARTH'S INTERIOR MAY BE FILLED WITH A **QUADRILLION** TONS OF **DIAMONDS.**

THAT EQUALS **TWO QUINTILLION POUNDS** (907 QUINTILLION GIGA-GRAMS), WHICH EQUALS **2.5 BILLION WASHINGTON MONUMENTS.**

IF BROKEN INTO **ONE-CARAT DIAMONDS**, THAT WOULD BE NEARLY **300 MILLION DIAMONDS** A PERSON.

THAT MANY DIAMONDS COULD BUY EACH PERSON ON EARTH **893 BILLION CANDY BARS, 66,513 ROLLER COASTERS,** OR 532 NFL FOOTBALL TEAMS.

INDEX

205

PHOTO CREDITS

Published by National Geographic Partners, LLC.

Since 1888, the National Geographic Society has funded
more than 12,000 research, exploration, and preserva-
tion projects around the world. The Society receives
funds from National Geographic Partners, LLC, funded in
part by your purchase. A portion of the proceeds from
this book supports this vital work. To learn more, visit
natgeo.com/info.

For more information, visit nationalgeographic.com,
call 1-877-873-6846, or write to the following address:

National Geographic Partners
1145 17th Street N.W.
Washington, D.C. 20036-4688 U.S.A.

Visit us online at nationalgeographic.com/books

For librarians and teachers: nationalgeographic.com
/books/librarians-and-educators

More for kids from National Geographic: natgeokids.com

For rights or permissions inquiries, please contact
National Geographic Books Subsidiary Rights:
bookrights@natgeo.com

Designed by Nick Caruso, Amanda Larsen, Julide Dengel,
and Shannon Pallatta

Library of Congress Cataloging-in-Publication Data

Names: Hargrave, Kelly, author. I National Geographic
    Society (U.S.) I National Geographic Kids (Firm),
    publisher.
Title: Brain candy 2 : sweet facts to satisfy Your curiosity /
    by Kelly Hargrave.
Description: Washington, D.C. : National Geographic
    Kids, [2020]. I Series: Brain candy I Audience: Ages 8-12.
    I Audience: Grades 4-6.
Identifiers: LCCN 2019035909 I ISBN 9781426338861
    (paperback) I ISBN 9781426338878 (library binding)
Subjects: LCSH: Curiosities and wonders--Juvenile
    literature. I Science--Miscellanea--Juvenile literature. I
    Children's questions and answers.
Classification: LCC Q163 .H2827 2020 I DDC 031.02--dc23
LC record available at https://lccn.loc.gov/2019035909

The publisher would like to thank Kelly Hargrave,
author and researcher; Grace Hill Smith, project manager;
Paige Towler and Avery Naughton, project editors;
Sarah J. Mock, senior photo editor; Molly Reid,
production editor; and Anne LeongSon
and Gus Tello, production assistants.

Printed in Hong Kong
20/PPHK/1

How
SWEET!